D1296796

BUTTERFLIES

INSECTS

Lynn M. Stone

The Rourke Corporation, Inc.
Vero Beach, Florida 32964

Edited by Sandra A. Robinson

PHOTO CREDITS
All photos © Lynn M. Stone

Library of Congress Cataloging-in-Publication Data

Stone, Lynn M.
    Butterflies / by Lynn M. Stone.
        p.   cm. — (The Insect discovery library)
    Includes index.
    Summary: An introduction to the physical characteristics, habits,
and behavior of butterflies.
      ISBN 0-86593-288-3
      1. Butterflies—Juvenile literature. [1. Butterflies.]
I. Title. II. Series.
QL544.2.S77   1993
595.78'9—dc20   89-32922
                                                        CIP

Printed in the USA

TABLE OF CONTENTS

BUTTERFLIES

People don't often think of insects as objects of beauty—until they see butterflies.

Butterflies are insects. Together with moths, butterflies make up a group of insects with many beautiful members.

A butterfly's beauty is not in its pencillike body, but in the two pairs of colorful, wide wings. Butterfly wings feel like velvet. The wings are actually covered by tiny, powdery scales that overlap each other like shingles on a roof.

Common in Florida and southern Texas, the zebra is a butterfly of the American South and tropics

KINDS OF BUTTERFLIES

Most **species,** or kinds, of butterflies live in the world's **tropics.** The tropics are the warm, often humid lands close to the Earth's equator. Even so, North America has hundreds of species of butterflies. Among the largest and best-known are the swallowtails.

The world's largest butterfly is a swallowtail, but it is not found in North America. Called the Queen Alexandra's birdwing, it has an 11-inch wingspread and is found in Papua, New Guinea.

Most swallowtails have long, stemlike extensions on their hindwings. They are like the sharp tail feathers of swallows.

*A black swallowtail butterfly shows
the wing tails typical of the tribe*

BUTTERFLY COUSINS

Butterflies' closest cousins are moths. Some butterflies and moths are very difficult to tell apart. Often, however, you can tell butterflies from moths by looking at their antennas.

Each butterfly and moth has a pair of antennas on its head. A butterfly's antennas are usually clublike at the tips. Moths usually have "feathery" antennas.

Butterflies are active in daylight. Moths are mostly **nocturnal,** or active at night.

A feeding butterfly shows off typical antennas of its kind—long with slender, clublike tips

FROM EGG TO ADULT

A butterfly begins life as an egg. An active, hungry caterpillar hatches from the egg. The caterpillar is the second stage of the butterfly's life.

The caterpillar makes a thin, plasticlike chamber, the **chrysalis,** around itself. Inside, the butterfly has reached the third stage of its life, called the **pupa.**

The pupa stage may last for days or months, depending upon the species. Sooner or later, a butterfly comes out of the chrysalis.

A monarch caterpillar begins to turn itself into a pupa

A monarch in its clear chrysalis gets ready to hatch

A checkerspot butterfly high in a Wyoming mountain pasture

WHAT BUTTERFLIES EAT

Butterfly caterpillars have jaws and mouths for feeding on plants. Adult butterflies, however, live on liquids.

The adult has a long, strawlike feeding tube called a **proboscis.** The butterfly uses its proboscis like a straw—sticking it into a source of liquid. Many butterflies drink **nectar,** a sweet liquid produced by flowers.

A giant swallowtail's proboscis probes a red thistle for nectar

WHERE BUTTERFLIES LIVE

The 15,000 to 20,000 species of butterflies live throughout the world, except on frozen Antarctica. In North America, they live from the edges of the cold Arctic south into Mexico and Central America.

Butterflies of one kind or another live in almost all types of North American **habitats**—desert, wetland, forest, meadow and marsh.

Within their habitats, butterflies hunt for certain kinds of flowers. A wild plant known as butterflyweed attracts several species of butterflies.

Fritillaries and an acmon blue butterfly (center rear) gang up on butterflyweed on a Kansas prairie

BUTTERFLY HABITS

An adult butterfly's life is short. The species that live the longest reach only 10 or 11 months.

The butterfly spends its adult life feeding, resting, finding a mate and, if it's a female, laying eggs.

Some species travel long distances to escape cold weather. Many other species survive winter by staying in the caterpillar or pupa stages until spring.

Butterflies have to be warm to fly. After cool nights, they must wait for the sun to warm them.

A butterfly's life is sometimes shortened by other insects—this robber fly's prize is a sulphur butterfly

19

MONARCHS

The dazzling orange and black monarch is the best-known butterfly in North America.

The monarch is about 5 inches across its outstretched wings. Those wings carry the North American monarchs on a remarkable journey. Each fall, hundreds of thousands of them fly from the northern United States and southern Canada to cool mountain forests near Mexico City. In springtime, they return north.

The monarch caterpillar feeds on bitter milkweed. That diet gives the adult a bitter taste that helps keep enemies away.

A monarch, wet with dew, warms up on a September morning

BUTTERFLIES AND PEOPLE

People love to watch butterflies flit from flower to flower. Many gardeners plant asters, bee balm, zinnias and other flowers that butterflies like.

In Mexico and California, large numbers of people visit the winter homes of millions of monarchs.

People collect butterflies for display. Dealers raise and sell butterflies.

Unfortunately, many butterflies are disappearing along with their habitats. Ten species are **endangered,** in danger of disappearing forever.

Glossary

chrysalis (KRIHS uh lis) — the pupa, or resting, stage of a butterfly; its outer covering

endangered (en DANE jerd) — in danger of no longer existing; very rare

habitat (HAB uh tat) — the kind of place in which an animal lives, such as grassland

nectar (NEK ter) — a sweet liquid made by flowers

nocturnal (nahk TURN nul) — active at night

proboscis (pro BAH sis) — the long, coiled feeding tube of butterflies and moths

pupa (PYU puh) — the stage of development between larva and adult when the insect is inactive

species (SPEE sheez) — within a group of closely-related living things, such as butterflies, one certain kind or type (*monarch* butterfly)

tropics (TRAH piks) — the warm areas near the Earth's equator

INDEX